GARSINGTON C.E. PRIMA

Dibby Dubby Dhu

by the same author
In Memory of David Archer (1973)
Collected Poems (1987)
Street Ballads (1992)

Dibby Dubby Dhu
and other poems

George Barker

illustrated by Sara Fanelli

faber and faber
LONDON · BOSTON

First published in 1997
by Faber and Faber Limited
3 Queen Square London WC1N 3AU

Typeset by Faber and Faber Ltd
Printed in England by Clays Ltd, St Ives plc

A CIP record for this book
is available from the British Library

ISBN 0-571-17999-1

10 9 8 7 6 5 4 3 2 1

Contents

Preface by Elspeth Barker vii

In foggy dawns 1
Who is Dibby Dubby Dhu? Who is he? 4
On a quay by the sea 6
They call to one another 8
Are you there, are you there 10
Sing me to sleep, you wild west wind 12
When Dhu rode in that morning 13
This line is written by the very hand 17
At midnight on the ice-bound Islands of the
    far-off Polar Seas 18
To me, sometimes, it seems as though 20
The Dobermann dog, O the Dobermann dog 22
Tom Cat Tom Cat 24
Among the Mountains of Spitzbergen roam
    the ghosts of the great Bears 26
The cheetah, my dearest, is known not to cheat 28
The Cow she is the Queen of Cud 29
Dibby Dubby Dhu, Dibby Dubby Dhu 30
This is a rune I have heard a tree say 33
What does the clock say? 34
A farmer stood at a farmyard gate 35

Never, my love and dearest 37
They lie beneath Old Fakenham Heath 38
Seven times seven sisters sat 41
'My heart is broken,' cried the Owl 43
Our little white rabbit 45
There is a lane that is lovelier far than 46
Call him gently 48
The house I go to in my dream 50
Have you been out to sea 52
Dibby Dubby Dhu rose one midnight 55
What shall I do today, Dibby Dubby 57
There by the rivers of India and Candia and Arabia 59
When I saw the Heron standing on one leg 61
Botherskin and Potherskin 62
What is the name of the tree where you live 65
My happy tree is a cherry 67
I dyed one April morning 68
When to Aylsham Fair I go 70
Stealing through the greasy streets of early
    morning in Whitechapel 73
Underneath a banyan tree with a rifle on his knee 76
Of evening in the Wintertime 79
I last saw Dibby Dubby Dhu 80
O Child beside the Waterfall 82
Gently now the trees are bending 84
Out of a star which may not exist 86

Preface by Elspeth Barker

George loved children and children loved George.
He was father to fifteen of them. The poems in this
selection were all written when our five children were
small. We had moved then to an old house in very
rural Norfolk; in our woodland garden was a cherry
tree and George's Dobermann dog scudded about
the autumn landscape, pawing the planes from the
sky and racing the wind; later he would collapse into
the baby's cot. Many of the poems were suggested by
things the children said or did or asked. Potherskin
and Botherskin are rabbit versions of our youngest
son and his best friend. Dibby Dubby Dhu, on the
other hand, is George's alter ego, protean and anarchic
as his creator. Exuberant or reflective, these verses
speak in the authentic voice of a poet who never lost
his sense of excitement in life, and who relished
bad behaviour.

In foggy dawns

In foggy dawns
as cold as yawns,
in pitch black nights
when no moon lights
familiar sights
as she rides the rolling sky,
in kitchen, garden and in attic,
as though my pen was automatic
I make these rhymes
and tunes and chimes
for several children. Why?
Because my head
is like a bed
from which at times
these runes and rhymes
get up and start to fly.
They whizz about
both in and out
they make my room so cluttered
(as I fell
down a wishing well
and all the wishes fluttered).

These runes and rhymes
and tunes and chimes
like gnomes and elves
disport themselves
on my bookshelves
in fours and eights
and tens and twelves
until I think that I'll
have neither chair,
chamber or stair
(and I've got many)
or table where
I can find any
room to spare,
for they'll be there
these rhymes like gnomes
these runes like elves
I make for children. I
think I shall run a mile.

Who is Dibby Dubby Dhu? Who is he?

Who is Dibby Dubby Dhu? Who is he?
    Is he visible to the eye?
If I met him one fine summer morning
    would I see him as he went by?

He may be the man with the mowing machine
    you saw at work in the park
with a battered old hat and a waistcoat that
    is not really up to the mark.

I ask you: Is he an Inspector
    who goes round examining things
with a little black book and the serious look
    that constant inspection brings?

No. Dibby is not an Inspector.
    Nor is he a District Nurse
although, my dear, like all Nurses he'll cycle
    through thunder and lightning, or worse.

Who is he, then? Who is Dibby?
    Who is Old Dibby Dubby Dhu?
Be careful for he might easily be
    the person who's talking to you.

(Myself, I think Dibby's an actor
    who loves nothing so much as surprises,
and for this reason, in and out of season
    he adopts multitudes of disguises.)

On a quay by the sea

On a quay by the sea
with one hand on his knee
sat Skipper ('Double D.') Dhu,
resting his eyes on
the far horizon
for want of something to do.

Up and up like a cup
that can sip its own sup
rose the tides of the turbulent sea,
but gravely he sat
gazing over, not at,
the monsters that gnashed at his knee.

The whales lashed their tails
like terrible flails
and the shark clashed its portcullis jaw;
round and round by the jetty
like a lot of spaghetti
the octopus rose with a roar.

Dhu sits and he knits
his brows as befits
a Captain among such a welter;
then he lowers his eye
and all of them fly
down to Davy Jones's locker for shelter.

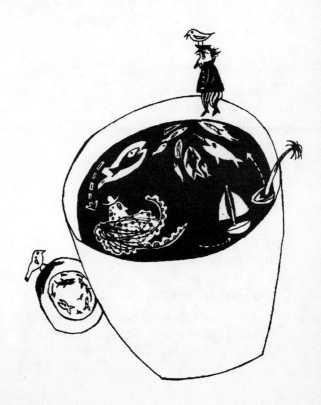

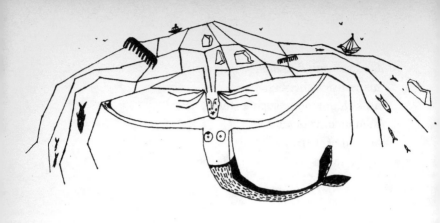

They call to one another

They call to one another
   in the prisons of the sea
the mermen and mermaidens
   bound under lock and key
down in the green and salty dens
   and dungeons of the sea,
lying about in chains but
   dying to be free:
and this is why shortsighted men
   believe them not to be
for down to their dark dungeons it
   is very hard to see.

But sometimes morning fishermen
    drag up in the net
bits of bright glass or the silver comb
    of an old vanity set
or a letter rather hard to read
    because it is still wet
sent to remind us never, never
    never to forget
the mermen and mermaidens
    in the prisons of the sea
who call to one another
    when the stars of morning rise
and the stars of evening set
    for I have heard them calling
and I can hear them, yet.

Are you there, are you there

Are you there, are you there,
Dibby Dubby Dhu, Dibby Dubby Dhu?
Whatever are you up to
Dibby Dubby Dhu?

'I'm a-walking on the bottom of the sea
with my seaboots full of sand and crabs and tea.
I've got so many fruits
and Christmas puddens in my boots
that I'm doomed for ever down here in the sea.'

Are you there, are you there,
Dibby Dubby Dhu, Dibby Dubby Dhu?
Whatever are you up to
Dibby Dubby Dhu?

'I'm a-flying by the rooftops of the sky
with my wings all cluttered up with apple pie
and because it's rather tasty
I keep nibbling the pastry
but if I fall I know that I shall die.'

Are you there, are you there,
Dibby Dubby Dhu, Dibby Dubby Dhu?
Whatever are you up to
Dibby Dubby Dhu?

'I'm a-lying in my good old truckle bed
with my trusty blunderbuss above my head,
but I'll never get to sleep
if I cannot count the sheep
that are nibbling at my toes right through the bed.'

Sing me to sleep, you wild west wind

Sing me to sleep, you wild west wind
    and I shall lie and dream
of huge white horses in the clouds
    as big as a ploughing team.

I hear the ploughboy shouting
    and the great horses neigh,
and above them the moon shining
    so white it might be day.

It shines in through my window
    and all my room is white.
O for the great dream horses
    that plough the skies at night!

When Dhu rode in that morning

When Dhu rode in that morning
    to Colorado Town
the blood and dust he wore like a crust
    cracked as he sprang down.

'I've ridden from Kalamazoo!' he cried,
    'over the Cheyenne Plain
and the word I bring is that Chief Eagle Wing
    will never ride again!'

He dropped in his tracks as he uttered
    those words that, in their fear,
the Citizens of Colorado
    had never thought to hear.

The Sheriff and the Lawyer then
    took up his prostrate body.
They bore him into the Bar and gave
    the Hero a rum toddy.

14

His red eyes, under the desert dust
  that wrinkled across his brow
Gleamed like embers. 'See! He remembers!'
  'Stand back! He can speak now!'

He raised himself on his right hand
  and with the left he tried
to stop the blood that fountained forth
  from the great wound at his side.

The whipporwill began to trill
  in a willow outside the Bar
and he heard the grey coyote dog
  crying very sad and far.

He heard the blow of the Navajoh
  as he struck with his painted hatchet.
What Navajoh could ever know
  the hand of Dhu would catch it?

He heard the Buffalo far away
  lift their great heads and mourn
for the thousand braves who found their graves
  that day at Powder Horn.

He heard the Wolf and Eagle weep
    for all that day laid low –
Sitting Bull, Bill Cody, Jesse James and
    Big Chief Geronimo.

And then it seemed, as in a dream
    he lay beside the bar
he heard the voices of his friends
    also from very far

Whisper: 'He's coming to.' And: 'Let
    the Captain get some air.'
'Force brandy down his throat!' and 'O
    where is the Doctor? Where?'

Dhu turned his gaze upon them all
    long, long from side to side.
'I –' His voice failed. He swallowed hard,
    so the story goes, and died.

This line is written by the very hand

This line is written by the very hand
    of Dibby Dubby Dhu.
It has signed papers, dispelled the vapours,
    and crowned a king or two.

Observe me well. I cast a spell
    (as you may sometimes see)
like the wind running over grass
    or lightning in a tree.

Mark what I say. For, night and day,
    I shall be marking you.
I am King of the Air, and everywhere
    I look for marvels to do.

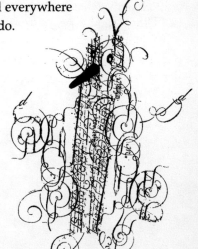

At midnight on the ice-bound
Islands of the far-off Polar Seas

At midnight on the ice-bound Islands of the
    far-off Polar Seas
I have seen the Penguins sitting with their infants
    on their knees
Lunching off a pair of kippers just as placid
    as you please.

Why? Because the Polar Region,
    where the snow falls by the ton,
Confuses all its native creatures, Bear and Penguin,
    every one –
Remember that the Polar Region is the Land of
    Midnight Sun!

To me, sometimes, it seems as though

To me, sometimes, it seems as though
I walked a world comprised of snow
as cheerlessly I have to put
one foot before the other foot
and find at the end of day
I have not got so far away.
It is as though I carried all
trouble like an iron ball
and nothing anyone can do
makes the world seem bright and new.

On such occasions I have found
it sensible to wander round
the farms and fields, and walk beside
the river where my two swans glide
and look rather closely at
all ordinary objects that
on happy days I do not see
because I'm happy being me.

But when the megrims and the gripes
and other rather dreary types
whisper miserably in
my ear about despair and sin,
why, then I go and look at all
the world outside my garden wall
and by the little river find
that fish start jumping in my mind
and flowers of every pretty sort
seem to wake up in my thought
and dogs I feel inclined to kick
proceed to do a funny trick
and horses by the fences neigh
at me in a friendly way
till all I see seems to be
determined – well – to tickle me.

The Dobermann dog,
O the Dobermann dog

The Dobermann dog, O the Dobermann dog,
O why did they buy me the Dobermann dog?
He is bigger than I am
by more than a half
and so clumsy at play
it would make a cat laugh –
he sprawls and he falls
over tables and chairs
and goes over his nose when he
stalks down the stairs.
He's the colour of seedcake
mixed with old tar
and he never knows rightly
where his feet are –
he growls in a fashion
to bully all Britain
but it doesn't so much as
frighten my kitten.
On the table at teatime
he rests his big jaw
and rolls his gentle eyes

for one crumb more.
How often he tumbles me
on the green lawn
then he licks me and stands
looking rather forlorn
like a cockatoo waiting the
sun in the morn.
I call him my Dobe
O my Dobermann dog
my Obermann Dobermann
yes, my Octobermann
Obermann Dobermann Dog.

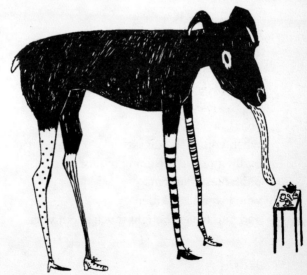

Tom Cat Tom Cat

Tom Cat Tom Cat
what are you at?
and why do you always behave
as though you had just
walked a long way in dust
to visit your grandmother's grave?

Tom Cat Tom Cat
when youngish you sat
by the fireside dreaming of nice
old ladies in mittens
who loved little kittens
and you never thought much about mice.

Tom Cat Tom Cat
the answer is that
as you get old but not better, a
fiendish delight
overcomes you at night
for hunting and stalking et cetera.

Tom Cat Tom Cat
I remember how fat
and full by the fire you slumbered
years ago, years ago
when the mouse did not know
as now, that its brief days are numbered.

Tom Cat Tom Cat
the mouse and the rat
at the pitter and pat
of your paw on the floor
like a large tiger paw
cross their hands on their breasts
in their shivering nests
and sigh with a fatal fore-knowledge:
'Is it us he is warning
this particular morning
he intends to dispatch with his porridge?'

Among the Mountains of Spitzbergen roam the ghosts of the great Bears

Among the Mountains of Spitzbergen roam the
　　ghosts of the great Bears

And on his back each one a coat worth an entire
　　fortune wears.

The Hunters from such shops as Harrods or the
　　Bradley Fur Trading Co.

Armed with howitzers and hatchets hunt them
　　down across the snow.

But the great White Bears are really ghosts dressed
        up in garbs of fur

And they flit among the ice like Northern Lights
        only silenter.

The Hunters, being simple, think they've shot the
        bears with guns and bows

When they come upon some fur coats lying empty
        in the snows.

They pack them up in crates and parcels, furtively,
        because they're cowards

Then ship them back to the Bradley Fur Trading Co.
        and to Harrods.

But the ghosts of the Great White Polar Bears are
        dancing hand in hand

Round the North Pole at Spitzbergen laughing fit
        to beat the band.

The cheetah, my dearest,
is known not to cheat

The cheetah, my dearest, is known not to cheat;
the tiger possesses no tie;
the horse-fly, of course, was never a horse;
the lion will not tell a lie.

The turkey, though perky, was never a Turk;
nor the monkey ever a monk;
the mandrel, though like one, was never a man,
but some men are like him, when drunk.

The springbok, dear thing, was not born in the Spring;
the walrus will not build a wall.
No badger is bad; no adder can add.
There is no truth in these things at all.

The Cow she is the Queen of Cud

The Cow she is the Queen of Cud.
The Pig he is the King of Mud.
Who are their Princes of the Blood?

The Princes are the little cows
And little pigs whose blood will souse
The Butcher in his Slaughterhouse.

Dibby Dubby Dhu, Dibby Dubby Dhu

Dibby Dubby Dhu, Dibby Dubby Dhu,
    are you an Emperor?
And if you are not, why do such a lot
    of people think that you are?

'I walk with the step of a seven-foot king
    and if ever I took a wife
she'd be the best Queen that was ever seen
    in any Emperor's life.'

Dibby Dubby Dhu, Dibby Dubby Dhu,
    are you a Professor at College?
And if you are not, why have you got
    so much extraordinary knowledge?

'I am as wise as an Ostrich Egg
    with nothing inside it but brain.
The wisest Professor is very much lesser.
    You see, I never explain.'

Dibby Dubby Dhu, Dibby Dubby Dhu,
    Are you in fact a Magician?
And if you are not, why do such a lot
    of people think that your position?

'My position is vertical, and I stand here
    tatterdemalion and tragic.
Well, not tragic, my lad. Perhaps a bit sad.
    Why? – No one will pay for my magic.'

Dibby Dubby Dhu, Dibby Dubby Dhu,
    then how can you be a King?
Since you have not so much as got
    one jot of anything?

'I am a King because whatever I touch,
    whatever I touch with my hand,
Gets up on its own, though it's stock or it's stone,
    and dances along the sand.'

'This is why I am an Emperor,'
    said Dibby Dubby Dhu.
'If my hand was laid on your head you'd be made
    a king with a crown, too.'

This is a rune I have heard a tree say

This is a rune I have heard a tree say:
'Love me. I cannot run away.'

This is a rune I have heard a lark cry:
'So high! But I cannot reach the sky.'

This is a rune I have heard a dog bark:
'I see what is not even there in the dark.'

This is a rune I have heard a fish weep:
'I am trying to find you when I leap.'

This is a rune I have heard a cat miaow:
'I died eight times so be kind to me now.'

This is a rune I have heard a man say:
'Hold your head up and you see far away.'

What does the clock say?

What does the clock say?
Nothing at all.
It hangs all day
and night on the wall
with nothing to say
with nothing to tell
except sometimes
to ting a bell.
And yet it is strange
that the short and the tall
the large, the clever,
the great and the small
will do nothing whatever
nothing at all
without asking it,
the clock on the wall.

A farmer stood at a farmyard gate

A farmer stood at a farmyard gate
with a hambone, a hare and a hickory plate.
A 'hickory plate'?
Yes, a hickory plate.
A hambone, a hare and a hickory plate.

What will you do with the hambone and
the hare and the hickory plate in your hand?
The 'hambone and'?
Yes, the hambone and
the hare and the hickory plate in your hand.

What will you do with the hare, hambone
and hickory plate that are not your own?
The 'hare hambone'?
Yes, the hare, hambone
and hickory plate that are not your own.

I will give them all to the poor for fare,
the hambone, the hickory plate and the hare.
The 'poor for fare'?
Yes, the poor for fare
on a hickory plate the hambone and hare.

Never, my love and dearest

Never, my love and dearest,
   we'll hear the lilies grow
or, silent and dancing,
   the fall of the winter snow,
or the great clouds of Summer
   as on their way they go.

Never, my love and dearest,
   we'll hear the bluebells chime
or the whole world turn over
   after the starlit time.
O not everything, my dearest,
   needs to be said in rhyme!

They lie beneath Old Fakenham Heath

They lie beneath Old Fakenham Heath
   the Highwayman and his Stallion
and overhead the clouds look like lead
   if lead can look tatterdemalion.

No memorial wreath on Old Fakenham Heath
    marks their obscure burial.
Not a stick, not a stone, nor, standing alone,
    a cross like a television aerial.

By the eerie light of the Michaelmas night
    folk hear this unholy pair gallop
with fading persistence as they cover the distance
    'twixt Fakenham and Ludlow (Salop).

By the light and the gloom of the thundering Moon
    these apparitions are visible
far, far off as they sweep on their wild way,
    rider and steed indivisible.

Kennelled dogs bark in the hogoblin dark
    and gentlemen reach for their gin
when the ghosts of Dick Slaughter and Stallion quarter
    a Norfolk that's blacker than sin.

The housemaids quail and turn rather pale
    and some hide under the blanket:
then they turn and sigh as the drumming hooves die:
    'Gone! And the Lord be thankit!'

Long, long they sleep 'neath Fakenham Heath.
    So long that the Antiquarian
mutters in hushed tones: 'Whoever stirs these bones
    is unquestionably a barbarian.'

And the ghosts in the sky of all their friends cry:
    'Where O where have you taken 'em?'
And the voices of Bow Street Runners reply:
    'To the Old Haunted Heath, Fakenham.'

Seven times seven sisters sat

Seven times seven sisters sat
   sighing in Salisbury.
The Man in the Moon looked down and said:
'Why are you sisters so very sad?
Things are never quite as bad
if you think of one thing that makes you glad
like the home of a friend, or a cake you've had,
or a fine brave Bagpiper splendidly clad
in a tartan bonnet and a Cameron plaid
singing out: "O I'm a handsome lad!"'

'Ah,' cried the seven times sisters seven
    sighing in Salisbury,
'Not one of us sisters would be sad
if it were not for the Cameron lad.
Yes, one thing alone makes us sad, and this
if you will only believe us, is:
we all of us love that lad, but he
has no time at all for us. So we
sit here sighing in Salisbury
with forty-nine reasons for being sad
and not one reason for being glad.'

'My heart is broken,' cried the Owl

'My heart is broken,' cried the Owl
    and the Moon answered: 'No.
Mop up your tears with a towel
let no broken-hearted fowl
rend the night with hoot and howl.
Mop up your tears with a towel.
    I am ashamed of you.'

The Owl repeated: 'Too whit too whoo'
    up at the angry Moon.
'Too whit too whoo, too whit too whoo.
It is all very well for you
sitting up in the starry sky
with the Lion and Seven Sisters by,
but down here in the haunted tree
there is no one else but me.
I can feel my poor heart groan
because –' he sobbed '– I'm so alone.'
The Owl wept in his bitter grief
and wiped his eye upon a leaf.

'Come, Owl. Come, Owl,' the Moon replied.
    'It's not as bad as that.
Lift up your head and you will find
stars all around you and your kind.
No Owl should ever quite despair
as long as I shine in the air.
Come, here's a slightly drier towel.
Cry Cheerio Cheerio, you old Owl.'

Our little white rabbit

Our little white rabbit, Lord, is dead.
    His killer was a fox.
He lies now in the everlasting bed
    of an old lettuce box.

He used to push a greedy paw
    through the wire of his hutch
until he got a carrot or
    a leaf or something such.

Dear Lord, is it possible
    that you, like us, could make
what might seem a permissible,
    a very small mistake?

There is a lane that is lovelier far than
    any other lane that I know,
and every evening, Winter and Summer,
    down that lane all alone I go.

It is always Springtime there, with white blossom
    foaming all over the bush and the tree.
And I meet, as I pass, many rabbits and piglets
    who never take any notice of me.

I shall never know the name of the marvellous
    small blue flower so plentiful there
I think it must be a kind of Forget-me-Not
    that no one has ever found anywhere.

I have never reached the end of this loveliest
    bird-and-blossom-in-Maytime lane,
for half-way I seem to rest and to sleep, then
    the cock crows, and it is morning again.

Call him gently

Call him gently
call him clearly
call him softly
in the night
call in chorus
all together
or one and one when
day is bright.

Call him from the
hills and valleys
call him from the
little trees
call him from the
fields of sleep where
all but he lie
down in peace.

Call, call him
from the happy heart
like a bird with
bright eyes

call him from the
sweet delight that
knows nothing ever
dies.

Robin, Robin,
lucky Goodfellow
I hear the children
cry
Lucky Robin
Robin Goodfellow
are you hiding
near by?

The house I go to in my dream

The house I go to in my dream
stands beside a little stream
full of dab and minnow and
trout I try to catch by hand
but every single fish is
more elusive than my wishes.

For every time I wish, you see,
I wish that someone else was me.
I stand and wish and call up spells
to turn me into someone else
but no matter how I try
I finish up remaining I,
however hard I wish to be
someone else, I am still me.

And so I think that I and you
and every other person, too,
must really be a sort of fish
not to be caught just with a wish.

Have you been out to sea

Have you been out to sea
Dibby Dubby Dhu?
Have you been out to sea
with your sea-boots to your knee
and your beard as black as tar
and your eye that shines so far
you can see Australia
and the terrible shileleagh
that you paint and polish daily
and manipulate so gaily
hanging down by the sea-boots
at your knee?

Can I come out fishing with you,
Dibby Dubby Dhu?
O I long to watch the fishes
swimming in their silver dishes
full of golden rings and wishes
underneath the table mirrors of the sea.
O I long to see the Whales
waving their enormous tails
like a flying Dutchman's sails
and the skimming fish at night
dripping fire drops so bright
as they swoop about in flight,

and the mermaids on the rocks
handing sailormen white socks
from a little cardboard box,
and the porpoises and sharks
giving off electric sparks
as they play such shocking larks
in the sea.

O Dibby Dubby Dhu
can I come out fishing with you
on the big blue sea?

Dibby Dubby Dhu rose one midnight

Dibby Dubby Dhu rose one midnight
   to sail his boat in the sky.
He knows that the stars are fishes
   and he even knows why.

Ask: 'Why are the stars fishes?'
   Ask Old Dibby Dubby Dhu.

He'll answer: 'Because they are silver
and swim about in the blue.'

I have seen him standing on tiptoe
high on the tallest spire
and even on top of the weathercock
to help him get up higher.

His long fishing line falls UPWARD
instead of falling down
and he sees the North Star twinkling far
below him in the town.

His old fishing boat is anchored fast
to the very tallest tree.
It bobs and rocks among clouds and church clocks
as though the sky was sea.

He fishes for stars and birds. And once
he almost caught the moon,
but his fishing line broke and, alas, he awoke
just one moment too soon.

What shall I do today, Dibby Dubby

What shall I do today, Dibby Dubby,
What shall I do today?
Shall I climb up to the hayloft
and hide among the hay
and let all the good little children
go to school today?

57

'Yes, let's go gathering coconuts,
Yes, that's what we'll do.
Let's go gathering coconuts,'
cried Dibby Dubby Dhu.
'Let's go gathering coconuts
on far off shores where wild macaws
dance in the ptarmigan trees,
and the Moon is finer than the Queen of China
and smells of Cheshire Cheese.
There, O there,' sang Dibby Dubby Dhu,
'we'll lie by the lemonade pool,
and in a wood we'll sing for the good
little children sitting in school.
We'll eat up all the bananas
and dive in the lemonade
and we'll live in a House of Marzipan
as fine as ever was made,
and there we'll sit together
on a chocolate piano stool
singing a song in praise of
all the good children at school.'

*There by the rivers of India
and Candia and Arabia*

There by the rivers of India and Candia and Arabia
the elephant lifts his enormous trunk to make the
      morning shadier
and then he lies down in the waters brown and
    dreams of distant Arcadia.

This is the land that has never been seen,
      O lovely, lovely Arcadia,
where the lion is mild and the tiger not wild and the
      Sun looks like a dahlia,
and there the elephant roams at will and everything
      is spectacular.

O every elephant dreams that he, yes, he in particular
will there make his home and find himself roaming
      the heavenly glades of Arcadia
with his trunk in the air like a parasol to make the
      morning shadier.

When I saw the Heron standing on one leg

When I saw the Heron standing on one leg
   and the Monkey hanging down by one arm
I thought: 'The two of you
   are so clever you could do
almost anything and never come to harm.'

But the Heron lifted up her silver voice
   and the Monkey muttered with his rubber lips:
   'When it's raining cats and dogs
   we gets just as wet as frogs
and we stands around like scarecrows, and we drips.'

Botherskin and Potherskin

Botherskin and Potherskin
    I will have you know
are large white rabbits with bad habits –
    definitely so.

Botherskin and Potherskin
    empty out milk pails
and then stamp large cream footprints
    all the way to Wales.

They pull up rose trees just because
    they like to eat the petals
then secretly they put back in
    a lot of stinging nettles.

Botherskin and Potherskin
    like nothing more than taking
jam tarts that cannot run away
    because they are still baking.

They climb up trees and fall from them.
    They do not mind at all.
Nothing gives them more pleasure than
    knocking holes in a wall.

They never wash; and they refuse
    even to clean their teeth:
and when a tree falls, why, both of them
    are sure to be underneath.

They tear up papers, they break glass,
    they keep on licking knives.
They have, I blush to say so,
    the time of their young lives.

I saw them not an hour ago –
    yes, I can see them still –
hotfoot upon some escapade
    over the little hill.

What is the name of the tree where you live

What is the name of the tree where you live
    Pretty Polly Parrot?
    And why does your nose
    try to touch your toes
    and why do you talk
    with such a loud squawk
    and why, Polly, why
    do you never, never try
    to spread your wings and fly
    in the beautiful sky?
    And why does your claw
    always want more?
    And why do you rest
    with your head on your breast
    as though you never
    lay down in a nest?

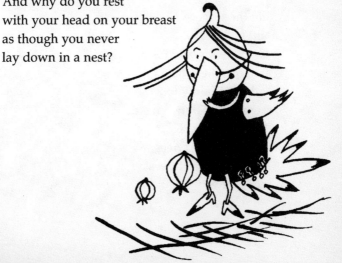

'I am far from the beautiful tree where I lived,'
    said Polly.
    And I dream all day long
    of the musical song
    I would whistle and sing
    if only I could,'
    said Polly,
    'in my pearly trees
    by the palmy seas
    of the gold and far
    coasts of Africa
    Zanzibar or
    Nicaragua
    or the flowering Keys
    of Florida,
    and there,'
    said Polly,
    'ah, there I would rest
    in my feathery nest
    and clasp in my foot
    the purple-skinned fruit
    to eat as I please
    in the beautiful trees.
    Ah the beautiful trees!'
    said Polly.

My happy tree is a cherry

My happy tree is a cherry
and I see caged within it
a little bird who sings there
every single minute
and the name of this little bird
is Lilywhite the Linnet.

O Lilywhite Linnet singing
in my cherry tree
when Mother does the washing
and I make the tea,
I hear you whistling, Lilywhite,
within my cherry tree.

I dyed one April morning

I dyed one April morning
    my hair a fiery red
for I had read that morning
    it's best to die in bed.

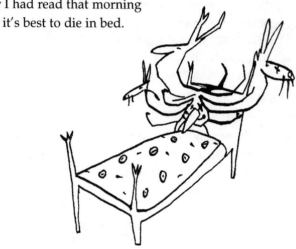

I lie awake of mornings
    I lie awake at night
but all my lies are laundered
    into transparent white.

I see the young corn growing
   and the summer wheat
but O I grow a better corn
   on both my frozen feet.

My hair has the habit
   of springing in the air:
I call it my jackrabbit
   rather than my hare.

O yes, my nose is very wise.
   I follow where it goes
because the pupil of my eye
   knows nose knows.

When to Aylsham Fair I go

When to Aylsham Fair I go
with sixpence in my hand
I with a cap and coat and tie on
and as fine as any lion
among the farmers stand,
I place my feet quite wide apart,
my hands behind my back,
I turn, on every horse and cart,
a knowing eye and frown as black
as kitchen coal out of a sack,
I stroke the great grey horse's back
and poke my stick in every stack
of straw beside the jumping track,
I glare upon the hunting pack
that shows its paces (rather slack)
by riding up the field and back
and at the Parson on his hack.
I stride among the little pigs
and scratch them with my stick,
I give them a few knowing digs
because I've learned the trick;
I wear a special ribbon in

the lapel of my coat
which is given if you win
anything of note
such as the Three Legged Race
or National Hunt Steeplechase
or a game called Tote.
I walk about with jaw stuck out
and shake my fist at boys
who constantly run in and out
making too much noise

because – I know from Farmer Prout –
this kind of thing annoys.
I make my way, at evening,
to the tent marked 'BAR'
where all the other Farmers
rather loudly are
standing about, legs all stuck out,
holding the jug and jar
and calling loud in fruity voices
and with the mugs held out,
yes, calling even their thin friends:
'Stout! Stout! Stout!'

Stealing through the greasy streets of early morning in Whitechapel

Stealing through the greasy streets of early morning
        in Whitechapel
an athletic figure flits with a red carnation in its lapel:
a topper and a white silk scarf adorn this elegant
        but elusive
shadow as it steals along, extraordinarily unobtrusive.

In his topper he conceals antennae and a radio phone
capable of communication with all
        Secret Agents known;
he is armed with a small Mauser
        inexhaustibly repeating
and a special instrument to stop rival Agents cheating.

Women cast themselves before him at smart
        parties in Seville
and, if spurned, retire to boudoirs and fall seriously ill.
Princes of the Orient have proffered him
        the Koh-I-Noor
but he smiles because he knows what they are
        offering it for.

The finest Agent of a Power no one has yet identified,
both Americans and Russians think that he is
        on their side;
yes, the President in Washington and the
        Chairman in Peking,
Anarchist and Anabaptist think that he will
        help them win.

He lounges in the Ritz at midnight, an
        heroic anti-hero,
Agent Dhu, International Service, number
        zero zero zero.
And in the interlunar spaces, as Dhu sips his
        tenth champagne,
the Martian Foreign Office knows that it must
        think again.

Underneath a banyan tree
with a rifle on his knee

Underneath a banyan tree with a rifle on his knee
    and a diamond dagger hidden in his turban,
in a caravanserai over which the vultures fly,
        seven miles from Timbucktoo
        sits Sheik Abadullah Dhu,
Lord of all from Marakeesh to Durban.

Not a solitary mouse in a mosque or in a house
    dares lift its head without this tyrant's knowledge.
At a word from Abadullah even those who've died
                     change colour
      for his reign of terror runs
      from the dying desert suns
all the way to Sandhurst Military College.

From as far as Wales or Wareham he steals women for
                      his harem
    and the caravans of India and China
pay him tribute just to go over Himalayan snow,
      or, if they think he's feeling

their money's not worth stealing,
they offer him a virgin's hand, or something finer.

But as he sits alone with his heart as hard as stone
        and his hands crossed on his rifle, not his Bible,
he hears, among the palms, Scottish voices
                                        singing psalms –
        he recalls how, after work,
        as a boy he prayed in kirk.
Dhu remembers, and a tear falls from his eyeball.

Of evening in the Wintertime

Of evening in the Wintertime
    I hear the cows go home
mooing and lowing by the window
    in the muddy loam.

In other places other children
    look up and find no stars:
they see tall walls and only hear
    buses and motor cars.

I love the muddy lane that lies
    beside our lonely house.
In bed I hear all that goes by –
    even the smallest mouse.

I last saw Dibby Dubby Dhu

I last saw Dibby Dubby Dhu
 sitting in a cave
washing his dirty shirts and socks
 in every seventh wave.

The clay pipe in between his teeth
 like an irate volcano
puffed out huge clouds of smoke that roared
 loud as a hurricano.

His eye flashed fire all about
 the rocks and wild sea lodges
like forked lightning when it strikes
 and everybody dodges.

He was, I saw, a Castaway
    upon an unknown shore
the sole survivor of a ship
    that sails the seas no more.

It was not in a dream or in
    a magic crystal ball
I saw him sitting by that cave
    with no one else at all.

But as to far-off Africa
    in a great plane I flew
I looked down on those desolate seas
    and there, below, stood Dhu.

He lifted up his searchlight eyes
    as I looked down on him
when, lo! he did a perfect dive
    and he began to swim.

I see it all before me now
    clear as I saw it then –
Castaway Dhu's return unto
    the Living World of Men!

O Child beside the Waterfall

O Child beside the Waterfall
what songs without a word
rise from those waters like the call
only a heart has heard –
the Joy, the Joy in all things
rise whistling like a bird.

O Child beside the Waterfall
I hear them too, the brief
heavenly notes, the harp of dawn,
the nightingale on the leaf,
all, all dispel the darkness and
the silence of our grief.

O Child beside the Waterfall
I see you standing there
with waterdrops and fireflies
and hummingbirds in the air,
all singing praise of paradise,
paradise everywhere.

Gently now the trees are bending

Gently now the trees are bending
    as the small wind blows:
when the summer day is ending
and the summer star ascending
and the swallow nestward wending
    home the shepherd goes.

Stars in the sky, shine down upon
    the Sailor and the Sea:
'I think that never a star shone
more like a crystal than the one
now sparkling through my window on
    everyone else, and me.'

Out of a star which may not exist

Out of a star which may not exist,
    across unthinkable spaces,
zooming through Nebulae which consist
of deadly thermonuclear mist
and veering between spheres that once
were Red Giants or Dying Suns,
    a single starship races.

Condemned for ever to traverse
the Circles of the Universe
in a vast recurrent pattern
from Sirius to the Rings of Saturn
and huger in its orbit than
the Ellipses of Aldebaran,
this lost ship of the Solar Seas
navigates the Galaxies.

Seated in remote control
like a god or a lost soul
goggled, helmeted and seeming
as though permanently dreaming,
voyaging through Triple Time

to the Relative Sublime
this Pilot of the Outer Spaces
conscious of the doom he faces
– Death, or a fate even worse –
bursts out of the Universe.

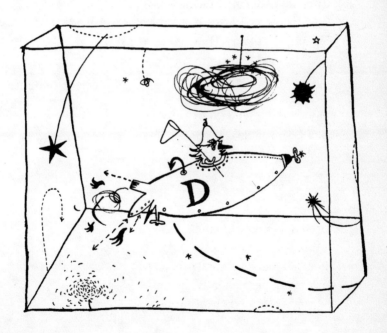

From far beyond the farthest star,
indeed, from so extremely far
that the radio telescope
of Jodrell Bank gave up all hope,
from spheres beyond the spheres we know,
faint and faltering and slow,
spoken with suppressed elation
came this last communication:
'I – can – see – Paradise – and – other – Islands.
Signed – Captain – Dhu.' And then silence.